twatwaffle

cunt Muffin

sweet as shit

SOY fucKiNG WHat?

Bitch, peas.

eat MY nuts

down for raisin some hell!

you Butter Back off asshole

you want a pizza me

til tHe SWeat dROP doWn

i donut give a flying fuck

KEEP YOUR HANDS OFF

flaky douchebag

in queso you didn't know

i'll have my cake

i'M SO fuckinG BaKed

YOU'RE a PEACH OF SHit

BiG fucKiNG diLL

i don't carrot all

CORNY BITCH

YOU'RE FUCKING KIWING ME

i YaM SiCK of YOUR SHit

one Salty BitcH

BERRY fUCKING annOYING

GROW a PEAR

WHat aRe you tacoinG aBout

hOt aS fuCK

piss off dick cheese

HOLY SHiitake!

fuck your fillings

Made in the USA
Las Vegas, NV
23 August 2024

94237676R00037